Undulations

selected poems

Undulations

selected poems

Martin Itzkowitz

ISBN 979-8-9957129-1-6 Paperback
ISBN 979-8-9957129-0-9 Hardback
ISBN 979-8-9957129-2-3 Ebook

Oh as I was young and easy in the mercy of his means,
Time held me green and dying
Though I sang in my chains like the sea.
—Dylan Thomas, "Fern Hill"

Contents

Turnpike

Night Drive

Night along the turnpike. Ann drives.
Bitter lights of Jersey blur in haze
Of bourbon drunk too late this afternoon.
Our son lies wakeful; his sister sleeps.
Outside, Elizabeth looms hostile, grim,
Towers burning brazen in the dark,
Fumes hung frozen on the winter air.
Within, slow numbness of a dull despair.
I reach my arm behind. Seth takes my hand
And will not let me go when I draw back.
My fingers touch his cheek and chin
—a moment—now—
My comfort is to comfort him.

priorities

out blue mountain tunnel into fog
but pressing on like pym
until it lifts at beaver valley:
a place to pause
as (riding eastward) once at winter dawn
the sun here hung a brazen gong
above the snow
sounding the silent heart
with its epiphany

now no tremolo at beaver falls
(paint bone plank flesh
fade soften fall away)
as college bells wring
in strict severity
through narrow gates
and namath's name's
a muffled drum
upon the cokeclose air

memory unpurged
of space or time
a turnpike turn's returning
no exit—no retreat

gateways

open roads   open roads
over indiana and ohio
go unbroken hours
of broken line
unbending
access limited
speed (radarchecked)
controlled

the dark conveyor slows
at measured intervals
a calculated pause to bolt
a sandwich or a wheel—
then resumes in regulated pace
eight-hour's computation
place to place
and reel to reel

descending imperceptibly from shallow hills
the belt declines below a leveling plain
an ear bemused with gearshum—
an eye with same
startle at the bounding of a deer
intruding music of a phosphorescent name—
maumee—elkhart—
linger on as afterimages
insensibly remain
then pass into distraction once again

gary's hieronymic flaming palisade
belies a frigid destiny of dis to come—
opaque chicago infinitely gray—the toll
of rigid harness and abandoned hope
easterly ordained now westward paid—
for this

bypath

The girl at a roadside stand in Michigan
Has cheeks as pink as peaches.
Fifteen, and far from Toledo or Detroit,
She still can blush
("No, it's not a wedding ring")—
Like apples now.
We buy a cabbage and some beans.
When these are gone,
The flush of sweeter fruit will linger on.

midwestern masque

3:18 in Lafayette:
a cardboard cut-out clerk
buckles on a broom
or bends counterpropped
above the register

a sleepless man
goes aisle on aisle
lids lulled by row on row
of vacuum tins
though still unsealed:

he pauses now
and one by one
reveals the mysteries
of orange pyramids

a pregnant woman ravening
delves through freezers
searches shelves
drums frenzied fingers
on a ledge then calms
to weigh twin possibilities
of lobster tails and clams

I pace my rounds
with empty cart
and keep a steady watch
for light: at dawn
all figures of the night
depart.

mph

at four o'clock
in west virginia
a woman leans
upon a hoe
head lifted
toward dark hills
in shadow now
the sun behind

a blue glance:
then gone as I
go on   between
white lines   drawn

she abides:
and will endure
her time until
she fills herself
the field she tills—
an earth's age
as bones compress
and more than now
field hills woman
coalesce

Occupational Hazard

Every day for fifty years
Salvatore Licari worked
At fitting pipes in public schools.
He paid his rent, then bought a house,
And later sent a son to State.
His income rose; his back was bent.

Now on summer days he sits
At public concerts in the park,
Listening while the brass band plays.
A finer plumbing than his own—
He taps his feet and claps his hands,
Yet measures with a level eye
How such twisted instruments
Should lie in clay or under stone.

alexandria

winter—scholiasts
clutch thin linen
to their nakedness
curl above scrolls
marginally
marking syntax—
none will read

in courts below
huddled sparrows
shudder at their piles
pecking chaff
for want of seed

long-threatened snow
now fallen
seems less rare

a cry of fire
smolders down the soul
ablaze
all couriers will swear
to foreign perfidy

still—antipater
his grimace half a grin
and furl-worn homer
left unparsed
stops scratching notes
upon tautogenes
and eyes a flaming sconce

—————

shopping for mother

polished pots in fixed array
belie pátinas of time—
purpose less
(just father and herself)
service for two
all otherware superfluous

pearl platinum precious stones
will not offset
rings and wristlets of her skin
and ivory carves itself
in jutting bone

house redone
in perfect readiness
chair lamp nicknack
wait in place
settled
as evening dust

a long robe is sure
to guard her flesh
against all whether

———

tastings

vintage

tuning
my tundish life
centripetal spillage
shapes the centrifuge
expelling sedimental ache
from whine.

connoisseur

too sweet for blood
your words upon my tongue
too deep for wine

––––––––––

cinemascope

sprockets worn
old film
jerks and whirls
soundwarped
waffling
gravel droned
in muffled drum
or smoothing
hoarsely hums
through scratch and score
in scathe that lens then
never saw

she sees
beneath all overlay
hears under roar
herself
as once she played

memory:
the last
of reeling images
to fade

a moment:
then hand
for nerve on nerve's
sheer chasm
gropes dismembering
in guideless spasm
voice rattles
unburdening
a wordless wheeze
wheels prattle
futile
in resounding
greaseless creak

no projectionist
(unseen)
dares choose
which frame to freeze
upon which screen
or cares

———

homages to hopper

shades

old men dun
at windows
of a dark
café droop
for light turn
one by one
a way to
bar the sun

swimmer

single figure in
a pool
pale yellow suit on
paler skin
against
too blue
within
a moment of
low angled waves

contiguous—apart—
bound only in
a common frame of
watcher's eye and
tile facade

server

chainstore
counterwaitress
slumps
among thin soups
not waiting
to sop spills
nor notwaiting

———

not quite autumnal

august
greenleaving
spreadpast
after noon
at edge
all red
or bronze
of sunburnt
sedge

no need
of hymnal
still sough
still waft
still shade
all birds
emboughed
embraced

on verge
x
septno v
ember
dearth or
dirge for
sapsong
earthswell surge

———

Dear Walt,

When I came to you in Camden,
To a frail house in a rotting street
Near a spoiled river,
A sleepy porter let me in—
For a quarter.

Your puny bed was much too small,
Even for your final shriveling,
And every jot and scribbling neatly framed
Beyond all order you had ever known,
Hat and shoes preserved in glass, past use—
He might have told me you were not at home.

We laughed together when we met outside—
You, somewhere, at my gloomy face,
I, for seeing you at all,
And at myself for having missed the place.
There, in the cracked walk, a clump of grass
Waved heartily, as if to say "Come in."
I spent a quarter hour in talk, and went away
Knowing where to find you when I came again.

—————

pas de deux

(after degas)

redrayonbreast
hung doublerowed
with plasticbrass
two sleeves beside
cuffs white depen
ding two brown hands
bear half a cash
mere coat light tan
and hold for sing
lesleeve to fill
pocketfumble
reachbehind with
pinkpale hand an
ticipating
calmcupped palm there
openover
handnohand touch

breast soslightly
waistbends blursthen
in othersrush
stripewine bareblue
tieshirt by now
lessenslarging
closepressed faston
glass fulfilling
tawnedge shade to
black ledge in thick
shut steelshine door
of parlor car

———————

Lincoln in New York

I. Cortege

> Cold, cold for me this April,
> and the rumble of carriage on cobble,
> rail upon wheel,
> jolts these new moldering bones
> in their slow journey homeward.
>
> Perverse geometry—
> no shortest distance between points
> but north from Washington to Albany
> west to Springfield
> and hypotenuse be hanged.
>
> Solitary—
>
> save at intervals along the track
> gatherings of folk in hushed hundreds,
> with rustlings of garments, badges, flags,
> and all bruiting baggage of mourning,
> with salvos of random cannon
> or tolling of woeful bells.
>
> Save for thousands in great cities
> along streets of the passing procession,
> my crate removed from the rail car

and drawn by cadres of horses
on wagons festooned in black bunting
to measure of muffled drums.

Or later, lid lifted in some public place,
face after face peering into mine
(who would have guessed so many friends),
some duly—some unduly—solemn,
a few like the fellow in Thoreau's town
(Hank once out of jail),
who japed at him through fingers meant as bars
and one lad with a thrust tongue
I might have moved to dress in other times
with a spoon or two of mustard.

Save in the long rolling spaces,
turned once again to freight,
I have for quiet company. our little Willie
in his own last quarters close and small.

But now just ferried in from Jersey
where a station clock stood fixed
at the fatal hour—
unless the fellow forgot to wind it—
unless the state's a place where time stands still—
I pause at New York's City Hall
and for some few hours am "at home."

Not entirely a jest, as having visited before
I'm more at ease than other bumpkins
with this place, making once the speech at Cooper
which, they say, made me—
("what I am today" I thought to add
but thought the better for decorum's sake)
and know a bit of Broadway—
a flake or even two of the upper crust.

And so they honor me today in all sincerity—
an old familiar (perhaps in Salem's sense)
if not old friend—with grief and fitting pageantry
considering their state and (lately) mine,
though just as heartfelt two years since
they would have had my hide.

We are all—it seems—emancipated now.

And here a chair is set—a throne more like—
all of flowers and empty at this hour
in token of my vacancy supposed.
I would not play King Abe—
and still am disinclined to such a seat,
though some might say—as ever—
prone and prey to stubbornest rigidity.

A throne of roses—not a bed
as Andy Johnson soon will find—
who might as well just plant himself upon it,
a random thorn or two in his nether parts
as naught to those well placed on every side.

Still, too soon for roses, out of joint in April,
greenhouse grown, forced before their time.

. . . . .

But now on Broadway rolling once again—
returning to depot and waiting train
an old rough in corduroy
bearded with wide-brimmed hat
(I'd swear I've seen the fellow once before
along the very street, pale eyes
for a moment locked on mine)
thrusts through the milling throng
to lay upon me—toss—a sprig of lilac—
heart-shaped leaves in season—
oozing, sap-run, torn.

Fallen—all impressions
faint—fog—fade—
save a photographic few—
fixed— as if in silver salts
and white of egg.

(I studied Matthew Brady as he studied me
and got the better of this horse swap—
a passel of pictures to his one).

Knox the Hatter, not quite mad,
sold me a top hat before the speech
then wangled my other for his cache
of headgear worn by crown heads,
wastrels, or celebrities to be—
on speculation I'd fit two of three.
Each man to his hobby so he ride no horse
Or set whatever cap capriciously.

Framed in a patch of windowpane
brushed free of fallen snow,
two Irish workmen lift
a pint of courage in each fist,
jig on sawdust carpets,
flushed with a coal-fire's glow.

Sorely tempted—still
I swallow spittle hard,
then turn away
toward that more sober hall
to which I go.

Mr. Bryant of the Evening Post—
great head, great beard stark white—
led me to a lectern of a winter night,
and later urged me free the shackled host,
inconsequent to currencies of cost,
spendthrift in the poetry of right.

Faceless gentlemen, six and more,
I know by billheads from each store,
As gowns and jewelry must accord:
Arnold, Taylor, Tiffany, Constable, Lord.
So Mrs. Lincoln on a spending spree,
while the brethren Brooks suffice for me—
well-cut, sturdy, no cause to complain,
save for one quite recent crimson stain.

Crossing "Beecher's Ferry"
to his Brooklyn church:
A fine sermon for fine people
in Sabbath finery,
well-padded in their pews,
while I in scratchy collar
squirm for lack of legroom
and endless thwack of wood
against less larded thews.

But later, on return, unwilling,
drawn to the mission at Five Points—
bringing to God this day

small children, tattered and ill shod,
thin with the gruel of poverty
in flesh and soul.

Pressed to speak—I let them know
I too had felt their pinch
of cold quarters, empty belly, public shame—
that they, like me, could grow beyond these
in some modest way.

What they truly heard I cannot say,
but in that vaulted place
I doubt they caught the choked catch
in my taut throat, or saw for all the dark
a trace of tears upon my pallid face.

III. At Cooper Union

1. Proem

Warm for a February night
if outdoors late snows linger—
warmer in this hall if only three-fourths filled—
warmest within this sack of an ill-made suit
(fitting, I suppose, for the ill-made man beneath it).

How shall I—scarecrow of the prairies
cadaverous and lean—a Scottish highland for a face—
crag, cavern, and thatch—
and voice in cacophonic squawk and shriek
to match the shrill of grackles—
for all long months of slow creation
win these heads and hearts before me?

I've half a mind to bolt at once
for the menagerie at Palace Garden
to croon and chorus with hyenas
in equal incivility—
or fly to hear some concert nightingale,
a Jenny Lind whose song might soothe
this uncouth breast to silence—
or as pathos suits the present hour
watch Laura Keene perform in *Jeannie Deans.*

Still—perhaps another theater at another time—
destined (as I seem to be) to stay
delivering this child of hard labor
and ushering, perhaps, some other birth besides.

2. The Speech

Mr. Douglas says, and I agree,
That framers of our polity
understood as well—and more—than we
the question of expanding slavery
into territories as yet free,
banning it—I say—by clear majority.

For of the thirty-nine who set their seal
upon our document of common weal,
twenty-three by common ayes and nays
expressed their understanding of its ways
in Congress, passing ordinance and law.
and all but two with neither hem nor haw
justifying federal domain in such a case.
Of framers who remain, near all—
like Dr. Franklin—one of note,
were in accord although they cast no vote.

And as to amendments five and ten,
both won approbation of these very men,
who surely with themselves must have concurred.
Not they, but slave-men and the court have erred
in misconstruing state and central power,
due process, owners' rights. But at this hour
acknowledging our nation must abide
the Evil where the Evil must reside,
we ask that all extension be denied.

Our party's purpose is but to restore
the framers' vision as it was before.
Confronted with original intent,
even Mr. Douglas must assent.

Southerners our party will accuse
of being sectional and claim our views
encourage slave rebellion or excuse
John Brown. Such allegations we deny.
Those who would the rule of law defy
are none of us. And slaves who cannot read
or hear our words can never pay them heed.
Our doctrine is to no way interfere
With southern slavery, yet persevere
Against its spread and bondage everywhere.

And in such enterprise we are at one
with Messrs. Washington and Jefferson,
the first in writing to young Lafayette
expressing hope that some time we might yet
achieve a union of free states, and signing,
in addition, several bills confining
slavery to current bounds; the other
urging slow release before we shudder
in prospect of a fury well assured
with Evil unrelieved too long endured.

And now, if they would listen—though I doubt—
I would address the people of the South.

I would say to them: If you are just
and rational, as self-proclaimed, why must
you violate all reason and its laws
when treating of our party and its cause?
You southern people hold yourselves aggrieved
because we will not share your misperceived
idea of right or rights. You would construe
the constitution as you please, in view
(without regard for what it fails to state
or to imply) of halting all debate—
as in Mr. Douglas's pernicious
legislation, labeling seditious
any censure of enslavement or aspersion—
the law proposed itself a clear perversion
of amendment one. But none expect
keepers of men would keep men's words unchecked.

It seems that rule or ruin is your creed,
apparent in your threatening to secede
should we at the next election claim
the presidency. Yet charging us with blame
for breakup of the union so foretold.
That is cool. A highwayman in cold

malice puts a pistol to my ear
and bids me yield or die, yet without fear
of contradiction, says that should he kill
the fault would then be mine for choosing ill.

Nothing, it would seem, will satisfy
except that we our principles deny
and join in opening the western gates
while rending constitutions of free states.

Duty forbids. To which we must stand strong.
As with life and death, twixt right and wrong
there is no middle ground. And divine intent
calls sinners, not the righteous, to repent.
Guided by our understanding's light,
we dare to do our duty in despite
of slander, threat, or fear. And so unite,
steadfast in our faith that right makes might.

3. Subtext

Half-truths, however glibly spoken,
lack eloquence of halves still left unsaid.

Wanting—mostly—full possession of himself,
what is a man that he should own another?
No matter the degree of his endowment
or cast of clay, each is equally the image of his maker.

No question then. We must contain this Evil,
allow it to consume itself then lie inert
upon a perished pyre, beyond all rising from cold ash:
a slow and smoldering season still,
down which generations more shall die
in forge-wrought chains beneath the lash.

Yet absent full resolve, a full assault seems futile.
And failed attempts must bring disunion surely,
democracy in disarray, a vision passing purely
to illusion— as if spectral smoke—
in validation of the long contempt
of hierarchs and kings,
with liberty of all— in every nation—
thus repealed, annulled, revoked,
and rendered less than dust.

Still, exasperate and irate,
Southerners might yet make good their threat to bolt,
and so unwitting wreak a rapid way—
should we prevail.
For we shall neither brook our dissolution
nor tolerate revolt.

Bloodier this course by far, for us, than slow extinction—
amends of flesh awash in driving rain of red atonement
for centuries of black men's thrall. A necessary purge—
Withal, is sacrifice sole means to sacred ends,
and those forever fraught with dirge and pall?

Whatever follows, there seems but small escaping
men at arms, and each of us, like them, a man of sorrows.

IV. Recessional

Returned to the rail car
(people pressing still on every side)
where our Willie waits in quiet chiding—
"Pa, where have you been so very long?"
We lie at ease in elsewise silent spaces,
shades of night ourselves in descending dark.
But soon to rattle off toward Albany
then westward on the final leg—
one—now more in earnest than in jest—
just long enough to reach the ground.

Still, in mind's eye, now, however dim,
a late image lingers and persists.

In a house off Union Square,
a lad at an upper window
asthmatic (it would seem),

weak-eyed, frail, precarious
sits leaning at the ledge.

An emblem of these very states
(Appomattox notwithstanding)
that owing somewhat to my late decline
teeter breathless on the verge,
fragile still with fratricidal fever
and internecine urge.
Eyes fail to see, shortsighted,
the looming trump of malice over charity.

Between late enemies, none—at first—
can reasonably expect a warm embrace.
But should a chill peace persevere,
we shall have schism frozen into place
and not reunion, with those so lately freed
returned to bondage once again,
fettered by old masters' new decrees
in unforgiving ice of ignorance and poverty:
enslavement but exchanged for peonage,
emancipation made a mockery.

I am myself no seer, vision blurred and blotted as it is,
but grasp at transient shadows
of a seeming hope for full recovery:
a doughty lad at last—stout, vigorous,
and breathing free—

a union reconceived in liberty, resurrected and revived
in that new birth sometime foreseen at Gettysburg—
a people—a republic imperishable—as one—
despite adversity——despite abundant trials—
despite all imperfection yet to be.

. . . . .

Now, the great engine steams—sounds—
strains—departs the station—
gathers speed—then levels to a lulling pace
with clatter on track, carriage lilt and sway,
as if to lids so surely closed might come profounder sleep.
Without, soft lamplight studs the New York night,
subsiding as we make our northern way.
No matter. Illumination of the common sort
cannot reveal my destiny dead on.
However bright they be,
torch and candle are of feeble use
against the starless evening of eternity.

september 11, 2001

in our backyard
white rose-of-sharon wither
fail and fall

as in red-berried bursts
of rapid fire
pyracantha flare and flame

defiant singeing
of autumnal air

lethal lashings
in the wind

toxic possibilities
defining a new season

———

Ars Poetica

untitled

writers o
f skinny
poems ev
en your l
ines of a
nemic no
meter ex
pand the
sense to

margina
l column
s space w
ell for p
oets and
peasant
s to know
your wis
dom lies

between

flatlines

poems postponed lie
past living grasp
in driftless piles,
blanched, dry, crumbling
at a mindseye glance or touch—
merematter, dust

still, heartslurk
in silent monument
pulseless, churnreft
like those of martyred saints
that will not burn

Bequest: Fragment of a Codicil in Which the Poet's Literary Remains Are Left to Science

And when you have me then in black and white—
A dot and dash upon a page—
And start to tittle with my jot,
There'll be a Freudian slip—
A misspelled word—a few,
Enough for just an article or two
But not a dissertation—
Though it will come to that before you're through:
One to fill an index, where a piddling peer
May read the title with a sneer,
While wishing that he'd done it before you.
And I, despite the strictures of my bier,
Will laugh in silence up my shroud
At both of you.

averse

donthink much
of poetry?

knowonder
it dontmuch
happen.

Harvest Home

Past three centuries
Of blight or fallowness,
The harvest comes:
Reckless of fences,
Spilling from bins.

With subsidies of time,
A poem's price is up
By half a life;
Upon exchange
The market holds;
Even England buys.

But rumors come
Of souls still underfed
For all satiety;

And questions rise
Of thinning soil,
And whether there is seed.

Agronomic doubt
Stirs economic fear;
Better hedge in prose.
Futures can be
No more than steady.

writ by rule and line

a moan
in mo
no no
nu cle
ot ic
sing le
syll ab
ic tone
a verse
can bear
no blood
to mar
row bone

___

y

e

l

l

o

w

leaves

of poets dead   drop before their time

three hundred years   through oil-thick

air

lie   smudgeward

upon formica slabs   in gray august

in concrete vaults   and no wind

windowpanes

are worlds of silicon

and motes within

care neither to

look out

nor in

———

psalms for the seventh age

driblet

old man sleeping
no tremor now
or tick of time
for slightsmile's play
on stippled lids
or slackblue mouth
spittlelipped for
mind's slow seeping

the view at long beach

sweat-suited, sneaker-lithe
a jogger pounds
his boardwalk mile or two
uneasily
past scattered flocks
of riven gulls
staring silent
from senescent rookeries

he fears their gantlet gaze:
though opaque as sand
eyes cannot see
beyond his moment's blur
against eternity

he circles, pauses, and returns

they wingless wait
for seamoil's surge
to brace or wheel or stave
as if in clearing
bottleshard or shell
along the beach
and sit in state
for highest tide
and final wave to reach

poste restante

in a doorway
set and bound
wrapped in
plain brown

and topped with
(nodding now)
a tuft of thread
an old woman sleeps

dreamless—
though her dreams
once white
as morning sun
shone clear
down caverns of the skull—
her vision of an afternoon
a dun and orange blur
beneath shut lids

parcelled light
precedes
delivery of total dark
to come

For K—

if i could go
behind your eyes
to splice the shorted wires
that spark the seethe and writhe
volcanically
and rock and spill
as slaver
and the loss of will

i would leave you
dawn to daysend
solder socketed
in steady light
no blackblurred memory
of dotted darknesses
before the fall of night

but unskilled unshod
in puddling pity
fumbling at frayed ends
i am more dangerous
to both of us
than all eruptions' ravages
or blacktape half concealing
what it never mends

Intimations of Breakfast: Unrecollected

What color is an
Orange
Juice drop dripping
A spot on an
Orange
Satin cloth spread in an
Orange
Sun
While with a
Peel-thick-lid-shut-
Orange
Eye I
Grope like an
Orang
U
Tan

———

Scotscope

Once in slate-gray Glasgow Georges Square,
As we lunched *al fresco* to the tympanned tunes
Struck by a military band complete
With drunkards' ballet out of time below,
A man perched solidly upon the bench beside us,
Dressed in drab, though starkly plumed
In least display of thick-cropped white, and glancing
A small and pale-blue eye in eaglescorn
Of pigeonpuffed and sparrowskipping play.

"The results of industrial capitalism," he said.
His eye grew sharper still; he did not look
Our way. Another socialist harangue we thought,
And sought to save the day by offering
Some food. A stare, a pause, our fare refused
In silent dignity. He spoke again:
The masters' puppets and the puppets' slaves.
One prances, one plays, and neither calls the tune."

Tolerant in his contempt, he smiled,
And at our next attempt broke bread with us,
Chewing to the rhythm of his thought
And savoring ideas an age away.

At last, past fruit and cheese, he let us talk
With him about the weather and our stay,
Noblesse oblige. But after biscuits when
Such themes wore thin, he grew content to speak
About himself, presenting us a portion

Of his history—no requisite
Or fee—outright largesse and openly.

Boyhood and young manhood in the mines,
He joined the union in the world's despite,
But left at length his coaldust camaraderie
For worlds of light and gardens' greenery;
Till hedged about with time and trampling tread,
Aristocratic feet on well-edged lawns,
The labor of his loins and sweat, he joined
The party, shut his shears, and severed ties.
For forty years he'd walked the Highland hills
(His face a rugged map of weathered glens
Marked with minute courses of the rills),
Staff in hand, alone, then with the woman
At his side, a deacon's rebel daughter—
Alone once more in wandering when she died,
A sole son gone pigeonmottled down
To managing a factory at Manchester—
And now, stopping every eight weeks' walk
At his two-room Glasgow flat whose halls
He shared with pesty hunger-scurried hordes.
But everywhere in talon grip he took
His book of poems, composed as if his heart's
High blood had pulsed through capillary nibs
Of zag-clawed finger ends—rough sentiment
In earnest sway—one a Burnsian
Lament for mice, prolific mothers slain
At his request, left to wander orphaned
Through the wearied walls.

He rose to leave, said nothing more,
But raised dismissing fingers regally,
Then turned and disappeared across the square.
We watched him silently,
Hoping the ratcatcher had paused that day
To chat with one so equally alone
Among unpeopled mountain caves or crags
And civil throng, yet knew that eagles dare
All height of solitude for sovereignty,
Though their mates be gone and nests lie bare.

———

Against Wrist Watches

If
I must be
Strapped to a sundial

Let
Me not be
Manacled to time

So
My arms may
Flail to free my rage

Though
The blade hacks
Chasms through my flesh

And
My heart still
Beating's ripped from me.

———

chaos

comes in soft malaise
as settling flake by flake
of sedimentary rock
in low lapped sea
or languid lake
which mirror brims slow ages
without flood
though drop on tepid drop
should trickle down or seep
dilute, dissolve, diffuse
in dilatory steep
till none are left to drown

and comes as well in casual cafes
where thumbs might rub away
old lipstick stains
on unwashed coffee cups
or not
and tarnished spoons
dip failing
once or twice
at shreds of insect wings
while filter lips
with half a smile
half-sift debris
at every sip

———

inclemencies

seasonal

cold front coming in
hard rain
high wind
driving bright october
down dark trees
toward winter
sheer slide
already underfoot
in leveled leaves

first frost

sudden cold
comes crushing
summerscrickets
stilling cricketsong
in crystal chill

February bus

sky of clay
mudplashed windows
filter faces spattered
brown or gray

____

One Man's Meat

At lunch after Petra
We sit with a family from Krakow.
"Have you ever been?" the daughter asks.
"It's a beautiful city."

Shall I tell her—
How one I knew in childhood
Fled that place—escaped,
Or that my father's father's village lay nearby,
Or that in Tel Aviv I'd met the last
Of all our fateful clan who stayed,
A survivor, with his wife, of Oswiecim?

Over hummus, we make small talk of travel.
"Next year," the daughter says,
In the Maldives."

———

postprandial

full bellied
basking
at indolent ease
maenads
past madness
leonine
casual
slow
lick shreds
of dionysus
from their teeth

———

Third Class Carriage

(not after Daumier)

In vestibules of ancient subway cars
Boys at eight or ten
Grasp seeming steering wheels
Lean or lurch with every swerve or sway
Transported in apparent mastery—
And more—past tunneled dark—
Toward visions of celestial planes or rocketry.

In vestibules of ancient subway cars
Young men just come of age
Brace backs against such wheels
To balance blind uncertainties ahead
While plunging on toward unseen destinies—
Or sooner—parry jolt or jar—
Times ruffling crossword ready in one hand
Pen poised unsteady in the other—
Lest stroke should smear or streak and answers mar.

camera obscura

in paleblue parka
sledded amid snow

a blackchild poses
for the kodakad

smile fixed as fate
alien among evergreens
foreign to frosthung flake

    in darkened rooms
    exposed

        in suppleplay
        to suns of home
        as tropicfronds

    old transparencies
    still lie opaque

———

On Contraception

vaginal jelly

strange napalm clings
but chokes with chill
till spermheads
stop their squirm
and tails leave lashing
to lie still

coitus interruptis

a multitude
of one
spurts
clings
dries
on torrid thighs
no dionysus
springs

Condom 1

"Do yer dirties boys, but keep it clean;
Grab yer bottle, grab yer 'ore,
So's they don't infect the corps;
Do yer dirties boys, but keep it clean."

Condom 2

Our water-tested love is sure.
Use two. We must feel—
Secure—and at the slightest pore
A life leaks through.

___

kinder-garten

sprite

a blur
of blondandblue
she pass
es overlawn
bare toes a
bove the grass

child about

battered drum beside
a building block—
shard of a morning's play,
living known in disarray—
scuffed shoe stuffed
with a crumpled sock.

then—at six or seven
boy amid borzois thirty deep
standing almost eye to eye and
lost in long hair—whelmed
with wet breath hot and panting
till led away to human crowds
and cooler air

now—three decades past
amid such crush of crowds who stand
but shoulder high (at most) to him
no panic, no presage of distress—
instead feet planted fast
and slow-drawn easy breath
both born of self-command

———

if a tree rises in the forest . . .

colrain, 2009

in the hollow of hills
— a cupped hand—
murmurs of makers
(call, cry, hosanna, yawp)
ripple—rush—rise—fuse—crash
from fingered peak to peak
sonata strain or symphony word wrought

then hush—all confined, contained—
save smallsound adrift in slow ascent
(wordwisps as if smoke)
sifting through slender space enough
between hill palm and thumb

who beyond will tell
windsigh from soulsough

———

Thanksgiving Hymn

Wild then, our first harvest's hunted token,
Ritual sacrifice to restive peace,
Advance atonement for all future slaying
Justified to God on prayerful knees,
For God's sake, *lebensraum*, or cash-hard ease,
Forgive us now we pile your humbled flesh,
This ignominious and ancient year,
Upon the board of our Thyestean feast.

Sailing into Plymouth Bay, our fathers
Bore the narrow poison of their aims,
Seepage slow, insidious, unseen
Along their generations' blue-thin veins
Toward rupture and the hemorrhage within:
Cabot to Kallikak, Bradford to Jukes,
With Usher groping down his fatal wall
Toward Yoknapatawphas of destined Snopes.

Benjamin Franklin, that manifold man,
Knew his Cotton Mather, read his Pope,
Tempered rage or reason to their use
Within prismatic or bifocled views
To build a school or start a fire brigade,
For which his library and name-brand stove
Were ready made, or advertise abroad
His daily or the new-found nation's news
By penny post. Yet gay enough a dog
At Louis' court, and once sufficiently

Bemused to send an emissary kite
To catch a star one dull and rainy night.
Exquisitely a man of his own time—
Not much beyond. Senile in '87,
His wild turkey offered for a sign
Of nation's honor, lay unconsumed
Upon the hour's altar, his own age
And the bird's, gone:

                    Resolving westward
Now in the wake of eagles, eye and wing,
Within a decade of the cotton gin,
A generation of the Mississippi,
Two of California's coast. All gyves
Fused in axle weld and rolling wheel,
Master's, slave's, settler's, earth's, tribe's,
All rebellion crushed in the grape of veins,
Salt wine spilling malignant rain
To wash dark soil down runnels to the sea
And leave the land perversely red and dry;
Vintage after vintage, thirst on thirst,
Till each man sucked his shriveled heart,
Or gnawed, or knelt to gilded calves
And struck at stones, or, blown
By funnel clouds to stagnant wells,
Murmured in parched cities of the plain.

Already in the fields of Pennsylvania
Desperate men go down their darkening pit.
          (*Wild bird, where are you?*)

Already rails across a continent
Bear their armored legions through the night,
Banners invisible as shade on shade
Descending earthward; while the stricken land
Lies pierced by steel stigmatic spikes
And will not rise.
          (*Wild bird, in what wood?*)

Already coffin walls of factories
Austere and indistinct from tenements
Hold migrant horde on horde drawn dreamless
Down long tunnels of their molish days,
Piston-pummeled, gear-ground, spewed for pulp
Upon the lung-dark air or thickened stream.
          (*Wild bird, hear my call!*)

Already the Great War and the greater,
Battle, stand, and skirmishes between
Or since; incessant, internecine coil
Of skewered flesh festooned on shattered bone,
Comfortless and charred, the staff and rod.
Now, within, the ravage and repine;

Clash of creed or color or class, lashed on
By an elect and corporate few, conjoined
To damn their reprobate and stiff-necked mass.

    (*Figured bird*
    On strut or spar,
    You are no bird I seek,
    No bird at all.)

This week the Babbitt turkey merchant comes
On yearly pilgrimage to Washington,
Knocks at the back door of the White House,
Bearing tribute of domestic fowl.
Wearing contemporary homespun
And official smile, the president's wife
Receives the gift and does not ask him in.

The Commander-in-Chief is out reviewing troops
On field maneuvers, and turning seer,
Foretells the Eagles fall before the Redskins.
No irony intended. Perfectly clear.

Shot down Wyoming skies for hawks or game,
Abandoned as banner and badge except in name,
Prophetic birds describe a double destiny,
Manifest: a sole, deserted eyrie,
A single egg whose shell is cold and crazed.

Late last spring the fledgling Toms were picked,
Big breasted, hollow-boned, all white—
Native woodland mottle gone; short heads
Low-slung; necks hung with small
But swelling wattles. All summer they were fed
On hormone-honeyed corn and left at large
Within the confines of their pen to tread
Whichever hen: But now in the solstice
Of the year, in ceremony led to solemn blocks,
Hearts carved whole and bled in offering—
Burnt, or wave, or heave.

At Sunday brunch cold leavings on a slab
Of bread will pass between indifferent jaws
Down gullets washed by floods of headless beer;
A vacant eye will stare at vacant eye,
An ear will almost hear the latest scores
Of ageless and interminable wars.

We gather—da dee dum—
To grandfather's house— da dum—
To hang this day our Quaker in Back Bay
And purge a soul at Salem for our sins.

———

The Body (Im)Politic

Bastille Day, Fifth Republic (1958)

All streets are still.
Though sentries stand on guard
Against opponents of an iron will.

And motionless, in shreds,
A tri-color flag hangs limply down
As if before some unseen resurrection
Of the Bourbon crown.

In his café
The Frenchman sits and shrugs
And sips his small despair.

Dag

Burst of a bomb, flash of the fire
And flare of the fall and the crash.
Steel-bird's-wing's rip bled flame;
Plunge then, and dash to the death
In crushing of bone and pungent searing of flesh.

A dove died. A dove died an eagle's death.
Red heart rose in the breast at the dive,
Soared at the smashing of steel, reeled,
Struggled to beat in the breadth of stricture and heat,
Burst itself rather than yield.

The Words of George Wallace (Or of That Ilk) Naked Before a Full-Length Mirror

Willie—Boy—
If you gonna be
As black as me
And just as big a sonabitch
As I am white--And just as rich—

Man—
Who in the sour-breath morning
Am I gonna talk to
When I stand here?

Season's Sonnet/Vietnam (1968)

Children of my syrup's ooze,
Caramel or clear,
Your tinsel flesh
Flares in a red ending
Of a flagrant year;

Sticking to fire
Through silence or scream,
To last quivering
Marrow jelly's ember,
Cooling of mucous eggnog's cream.

"The flesh rises; the flesh falls."
For cause:
Green plastic wombs'
Masked menopause,
Hollows of popcorn balls.

Czechoslovakia (1969)

"I'm all right," she said,
Though few had asked
And none had moved to help her rise.

Then, struggling to her feet,
She nearly smiled
And lightly brushed a hand across her eyes.

"I'll be fine," she said.
The voice was calm,
But quavered with her stifled cries.

In her pain, she raised
The skirt-shreds to her knees
And wiped her bloody thighs.

second attempt[1]

stilled long decades
ancient evil raging
ravening returns
stirs the soul
of stauffenberg
in endless sleep
remembering:

no weakened weapon
moved by chance

no bar of oaken
table top or leg

no failure this time
(if further east—or west)

20 july is fitting
but justice deems it done
without delay

n. amerika: final declension

amass   amorphous
amalgam   amuck
amiss   amort

———

Rites of Passage

From where they stood, leaning on their tools
in the tunnel, and leering under rims
of domed and rigid hats, beer-bellied
and bicep-bulged, they hardly saw
an extra inch or two of platform thighs,
firm and mini-skirted over patent boots:
Enough for "Chocha!" calls and "Pussy!" hoots;
Only roundings of an underbreast,
and that the sweater neckline must be low,
a chain, though not the furrow-mounding flesh,
revealed and plainly set with crucifix:
Enough for "Great Boobs!" "Hooters!" "Tits!"
Visible, a face of tan-smooth skin
with mouth a pink-cream smear
and eyes outlined in black and shadowed green.
But pupil's stare unseen, nor iris flecks,
Nor nostril's flare, nor mark, nor hair awry:
Enough to suck in lips and stroke a fly.

When she boarded her train on the opposite track,
they bent with bullock-necks above their toil,
Saint Christopher suspended at their chests,
and struck with pickaxe point or thrusting spade,
blow on grunting blow upon the bed.

———

Produce

Figs in greening feel to full is all,
Swell-golden, flush, and fall,
Juice-laden, lush—
Peel-parted flesh
Bare to beesmouth or bird
Till honey-prod
Tonguing or beak
Pulp-seed and pour
Whole in a pulsing air.

Figs in fullness fear that green was all,
Cleave though leaves fall—
Lovers—cower, cling
Through a gorgeous hour's gleam,
Linger, dull, languish
Past prime, bear anguish
Of bare time, till hung
Brown-rivelled, core-crushed, and strung
Down from a twisted string.

---

arboricide

ripped from their rooting
peach trees now unpurposed
spread and splay at random
limbs whichever way
all fruitless flailing ceased
long unflowered, left unleaved

skeletal, twisted, gnarled
they are not piles
of butchered bones
at buchenwald

nor ashen agonies
held captive
at pompeii

nor arthritic dancers posed
fantastic by some mad degas
in mock ballet

not nearly like the least of these
nor very far

———

pastoral

name upon wind
you come delicate hoofed
nuzzling an ear

light-through-shook-mane-
handstouch-to-flanks-
in-quiver play

till high-wined laugh's bluebolt
giftapple mouthed like a rose

———

Japonaiserie

a fallen moth's faint flutter—
perhaps the wind

song sprouting in my heart:
green rose, crimson grass

mine:
thick listlessness
of wet wash tumbling
through public machines
unwrung

peter, paul abide
steamgratefully
beside the worship house
unchurched

hair on lips of urinals:
shedding of illusion

———

Camille Pissarro at the Hôtel du Louvre

Confined to quarters, as if I myself were being tried
and not the harried captain—innocent upon the very evidence
(no mere opinion held by prejudice of common race).
Zola himself proclaims it at long last!

Voices now envenomed by Degas' old rant,
renewed in dotage but grown more intense,
and tainted with Renoir's infirm assent,
the mob howls for the writer's blood as well.

I am at risk to show my Jewish face.

Confined—cut off—an ancient story:
great-grandfathers forced to feigning Christian faith
among the Portuguese—parents severed
in St. Thomas from the *corps juives*
(their marriage contravening Moses' law)—
and they themselves from me—a paradox—
for embracing my alien Julie.

An antique story of the race itself
but here—with me—no wandering:
in this apartment–fixed—immobilized—
immured in yard-thick walls.

Still, my cell is less a convict's than a monk's,
no mere seclusion in the sacred work
so long as paint and brush and canvas last.
The clarity of window glass frames scenes
of horses, people, carriages, and trees
that rise like incense from the streets below.

Yet something stirs—other than the eye—
draws the image to me, stretches, strains
past imperfections of the panes toward truths
deflected from the vision I've held true.

I recall a painting—glimpsed but once—
by Van Gogh's brother (Gauguin's half-mad friend),
hear vague reports of soaring images in bronze or stone
too smooth to credit a Rumanian peasant's hand,
a traveler's rumor of a child with colored chalks
tracing long, lean forms on narrow sidewalks at Livourne—
perhaps—Jewboy that he is—a second coming—of myself.
Still, doubtless this is true: for all it shatters,
light in prismed lives no less beams through.

———

lebensraum

grey house
settling

sags
weathers
wears

cracks
in character

bay
gable
eaves

rare

mid
flat facades

the charm
the charm

the vacancy

Relics—for FJ in Memoriam

dead in desert spaces
corpse to flames consigned
she left behind

parched cartons of pale pages
bound, bleach-bone white, all
breathless in each corrugated pall

unlike whose they were
such stuff must burn
sans mourner, sans eulogy, sans urn

———

thirteen ways of (not) looking at a jailbird[2]

1. Gary Gilmore
Hewont Kilmore

2. uncivil right affirmed
by court decree
noman need be
appealing

3. I hate my life
but—oh—U—
TAAAAAAAAAAAAH

4. after mountain dew consideration
the warden hung his soul upon a hooker
by all accounts coopting for survival

contracts out at less than scale
he picked his five scabs nervelessly

5. two rival bands
protestors on parade
borebanners:

an eyepatch for an eye
a jawbone for a tooth

6.   "Dominus vobiscum." (The Lord be with you.)

        "Et cum spiritu tuo." (And with your spirit.)

        Ouchetay! (Touché!)

7.   "Let's do it."
        the DEED
        an inter
        National Lampoon

8.   "Guess he lived two minutes till he died;
        Least I couldn't find a place to put the 'scope'."
        Hard to hear a heartbeat where a heart had been.

9.   in her mobile home
        his mother sat
        arthritic, unmoved

10.   five men go in utah
        none can see
        invisible for hoods
        they do not wear

11.   "My nephew died in dignity."
        strappedshrouded
        targettagged
        he did notcry
        uncle

12.   Awn a grahy 'n' early mornin'
        Gary Gilmore met his fahyte
        Shot t'death in Mountain prizzun
        Bah the hahrd guns of the stahyte

        Of the stahyte—of the stahyte
        Bah the hahrd guns of the stahyowrghhlnk

13.   until tomorrow's execution
        this is whelan wein speaking

        g—a—r—rrratings
        y—g—i—iiincome
        l—m—o—r—e

———

In Brief

false messiah

struck squirrel
stunned in certainty
stirs a gray tail
warding off or welcoming
a second coming
of the wheels

imitatio

flies survive
in corners
in december
hovering over tables
too close to toilets
rising buzzing
dropping to crumbs
like LADIES and GENTS

scholarly pursuit

in search of an answer
for which there is no question
no sage, doubtless,
will pause to ask direction

any philosopher to any waiter

moldy truths
crumble on tongues
melt to mush
at touch of toothless gums
better bring
whose mouth is dry
and full of fangs
a platter of fresh lies

dumbshow

              ape
        with punctured cup
      bows nakedly and bends
           cavorts

                      at loose and longleashed ends

              none
         passing by attends
              discerns
         the timeless tune
       a handless hurdy-gurdy
             turns

epochgram

kinky chryseis
goes swell-bellied
having stooped
to flagelation
by a sperm

fabrication

it's hard to tell
if lies of youth
are worse
than lies of age
--or the reverse--
and that's the truth

optical illusion

seventy
in mind's eye
turns to seventeen

lines of time
erased
firmest flesh
for sagskin hollows
all replaced

a blink
then vision gone
without a trace

Joan Baez

interlochen, 1998

no longer jeans or swirling skirt
new-fashioned note of silken scarf
about her throat
a splash of lavender
against the black
of knee-length pantsuit
stark and curt

silver bangled, silver haired
(such turning in the teem of time)
a style less spare
gone a lone guitar
a single chair
instruments now amplified
a stage now shared

old songs, old causes lost or won
recede as echoes of an ancient strum
fresh currencies ascend like larks
exultant in new threnody or thrum

still thriftless, still unspent,
an art, a soul unriven--
still twin treasure
blent and driven:
her golden tone, her ruby heart.

Hawk Mountain

Wakening before first light
They climbed the rugged trail to north peak
(Painted markers pointing out their way)
To glimpse an eagle in full sweep
Along the Kittatinny range—

And past noon still strained eastward,
Glasses molded to their hands
Or legs braced against a tripod frame.

"It doesn't get much clearer," someone said.
Below, a brown stream made its slow
And muddy way through leveled fields.
Sun had not burned off the haze.

Late in the day, one with nylon vest
Bore rumors of a sighting southward:
Murmurs of his listeners died away.

No eagle came.

Two red-tails circled the valley,
Then disappeared below the western ridge.
Once, toward evening, a lone osprey hung
Upon the wind with spread wings
And dropped to the gray limbs of a dead tree.

icons

children pack guns with their lunch on the plains of Kansas

(auntie em turns tricks
                on a 900 line)

children flash guns on their bus on the plains
                of Kansas

(toto writhes without eyes
                on a black-candled altar)

children blast brains in their schools on the plains
                of Kansas

(dorothy lies
        sodomized
                in a shallow grave)

———

Two

The plastic handle of an attaché
Cuts through calluses,
Aiming for underflesh,
Intent on bone.
Anesthetized with newness
And a need to hold,
The hand knows nothing,
But wonders why its palm is dry.

A leather handle raised the calluses
While grasping rubbed a hollow in the grain,
And flesh in folding worked the hand to wet
Soaking tanner's chestnut with a deeper stain
And it was even whether man or thong
Would wear away or last.

I have in mind
The coated edge of razor thighs
Indifferent as it scrapes another skin;
Series circuitry of switchedon hair
Shorted to discharge without light;
Anvil bellies of those
Who bear unmarked for rubber shields
While hammer after hammer breaks unheard
In polyurethanic atmospheres.

I have in mind old lovers' intimations eye in eye
Or same-talk in the sharing of their lives,
Deep and equal breathing in the fall
After slow-fused passion of the rise,
The comfort of men coupling—
Shaped, shaping their easy wives.

————

Allure

Come with me to the gardens of Rousseau,
Where monkeys hang like golden lamps
In shimmering trees,
And lions sleeping among orange flowers
Breathe music through strings of lutes
Left by Roma.
Lie with me in the gardens of Rousseau,
In the green night,
And there be true to me.

———

Reflections of Professor Bluestone

Peering at the pages of a book—
Old photographs of European Jews—
Those shades of time that God and men forsook—
And searching them for blear-eyed blur-edge clues
Of lineage or most familiar look,
I saw but faintest traces to confuse their lot with mine—
Although the heart mistook a half-smile,
Faded now, for dimmer views.

And who envisioning their life of rote,
With poverty and prayer in common sway
Toward common destiny obscure, remote,
All-staring eyeless in the gaze of day,
Would blindly choose to see himself a mote
In monochrome of vaguest brown or gray?

Though—when this morning's mirror-steaming spray
Condensed opaque upon the glass, and smote me there,
In clouds obliterate as they, illegibly, I scrawled
A mental note: As eye may *was* distort, I *shall* betray,
What razored hand is looming toward which throat?

———

auditions

antiphon

the metaphor of mumble
is a sound
mute in a muffle of molars
dripped on a loose lip

a profound rumble
of lung
too lightly hung
on too taut throat strings
springing to motion
but unsung

a meaning of means unknown
none asunder
neither over under
but the tone

sounding

silent screams
equally atone
for deafened ears
utterly at one
no medium no means

forte

soul-skilled fingers
rousing steel to sing:
what songs of flesh might rise
to equal fingering?

of note

accord
this minute
diminishing
dim innuendo

The Reading

Behind the curtain of light descending—
Behind the lectern—
Behind the page—
Behind his own eyes—
The poet speaks at four removes.

Haloed in the legend of his race—
Wreathed in his own fame—
The critics' anointed performs
His sacrament of public reading—
Communion of wafer thin pages
Dunked in a southern whine.
Only half divine,
He breaks the circle of his soul,
Taking the flesh of other men—
A revelation of the life they share—
But knows that men will have their god
And kill him too.
Above them, on the stage,
He strikes his pose,
And yards from the nearest one
Plays Abraham and Isaac—
Father and son—
Adam, altar, and ram.

In blue suit and striped tie
He fumbles to unzip his fly,
Lets his dong dangle,

Invites the world to take hold,
And tells how in in a junkyard once
He used his tool to monkey
With a wench who came for screws.
Down home they ran a still;
His brother-in-law has gone to booze;
(Knee slap, wink, headhang and smirk)
He's also fond of zoos.
"Cat house" (laughter, pause)
A spotless leopard's a pander
To rib-rub, sole-stroke—
Back-of-the knee-jerk—
(Off).

II

Seven poems in an hour—
Less than a hundred lines—
Scattered through speeches and laughter,
Read quickly by a hunched man
Half crouched behind a stand,
Who snaps his thread with a snicker
Or comic shake of his head.

At the end there is applause,
Though less than for
His easy patter and homely saws;
They hear him darkly

through a shield of light, a wooden wall.
His living image hovers at the ear
And casts its pall.

In gathering of books and coats,
Shuffle of retreating feet,
An unasked question "What was it he read?"
Will pass with smoothing of a brow
To pleasure: "Remember when he said . . .?"

III

And are you mine—stiff upon the page—
Laid out in printer's measure—
Embalmed, jacketed, and bound—
Stark black and white?
And am I,
Your coffin resting on this catafalque
Reading you here, your own eulogy,
A proclamation of my life
Before hired mourners
In pantomime of sacred rite?

Lovely in the mindsoul once
As after I lay long coupling
You sprang and writhed to shaping
In friction of the phallic womb—

Lovely in expectation—lovely in agony—
Now complete—you lie
My stillborn child.

But there's a pulse that was not mine—
A cry of life inflicted at strange hands—
And in the sweet room where it thrives,
Strange breath passes membranous
Through gauze-thin masks.

Flesh bleeds. I cannot feel
The pain or flowing blood.
Cast in my image—the living form your own—
I see the wound—I cannot heal.

Though—as dying then to me
And quickening toward friend and lover—
I wept that you should go.

IV

Lights dim,
Backs of necks ache for looking up at him,
Ears strain their obeisance to the poem.
Tragic relief—a laugh's lull
In a comic leitmotif—
The mouth maintains its tone.
But he has known himself—

Has cut his flesh
To suck a rattler's venom from his veins—
And in the flow
Of Abel's self-drawn blood
Has washed the hands of Cain—

Has know Gomorrahs of back road motels,
Where once a week a man and woman came
To spend an hour in Jerusalem
Under calendars and cattle on the walls.
Eyes pass from page to hall—
Word from eye to brain, larynx and tongue—
Lips spew peelings of bruised fruit,
Whole in the mindsoul once,
Once at the heart's ear hung,
Now at the microphone mute.

Crowned in kilowatts—
Enduring stigmata of applause—
His own sweat and drool—
He stands and reads.
Within—cool loam stirs
At recollection of first light—
And silent glory of the seed.

In the Museum

Mimicries of men survive in shards,
Or clown at length without an arm or head,
And even perfect busts are mocking parts;

But things that never were—a jug or jar—
Seem whole; cleft or scarred,
They still preserve the mien of stone,
The calm of clay, unmarred.

———

Isaac

Numb fingers fumble at the flesh
But cannot tell for muted touch
The sheep from shepherd,
Nor blind nostril smell the sheep from man;

Nor leaden sockets screw their shattered lamps
To sift the dark from fair, nor inner ear
Discern an equal drift of bleat and bark.

What wonder then—
The dying man gasps "Esau!"
Grasping Jacob's hand?

U-turns

To My Student I Would Not Destroy (S. L. S.)

I would not do
the death of you,
heave a hand-
book hafted helve
of rule or rod,
crush with crude,
cleave, delve
the frail sod
of your living's shell.

Stir then.
All ready
bright blood grips yolk,
spins strength,
spurs and gathers to pulse;
Fill—Full—
I will bear
shard-stroke-witness-burden—
Burst.

Fledged—free—
of an own-wing's flight then
Be.
I, trembling
in your sky-arc soaring's wake,
will sing,

bond-breach of time or cage,
new praise—
Fly—Reach
an utmost eyrie—
Cling—till we
each-plunge, rivet and raise
with shining fishes from the sea.

asian studies

wearied with reading
i lift my troubled eyes
to where in sofa'd sleep
she lightly lies—
a daughter of japan—
head—canvas-backpack cushioned
skirt summersheer
foot—sandalshod

until she stirs, wakens,
leaves in nimble stride

my leaden gaze
drops pageward:

once more
the flash, blaze, char
a slakeless thirst
a skin unfleshed
flame flayed

widows' memories
of hiroshima

dysconnect

back to back to back
in severed solitude
bent above
small screens
ear blue-tooth pierced
as if with awls
of ancient servitude
they reach toward worlds
remote: oblivious of
each to each to each

Rhetorical Question

My students, my shards,
How shall I whole
In the heel of time
Such desperate parts;
Or sow hale seed
In seasonspace
For tareworn soul,
Or make amends
Of threadbare grace
To tattered hearts?

Wheels

Briggs' motel is on the left now,
Whaley's tavern on the right,
As we return--
Gone weeks or months or days.

Evergreens go by, preserving constancy.
Which moves, we or they?
Others turn in leaving,
Steadfast in the circling of their ways.

Sunspin, earthswhirl, moonsrise or wane,
Seasurge and spill unceasing:
Ebb to flood to ebb to flood again.

───────

dancers

aged injured
fit to cane
or chair
dancers still
in memory
move to
melodies
unheard
turn perfect
leap rare

——————

Ecological Observation

Washed up by spring rain,
A worm, now dry and curled,
Lies in carrion heap,
A half-inch piléd feast
Which servant ants set humbly,
Course by course, before
Their throned and tunneled queen;
An ordered paradox:
That one who rose to die
Should fall so soon, so high.

———

Exeunt Omnes

Mutual Reflection

A yard and thirty years apart, we sit
Through surface silences before the last—
One large and sprawling, the other sunken, shrunk—
And look away to where the late sun casts
Our images upon a distant glass.
Heads half illumined in the passing light,
Our gazes meet, hold fast, profoundly dumb,
Fixed in recognition of what one had been,
Of what the other would in time become.

Sophocles at 90

Charged with senility,
I read to them
my last of Oedipus.

Cleansed, we go now,
he and I,
clear-visioned

(sight rent)
toward Colonus
and the sacred grove
of our ascent.

Passing Pompton Lakes

here an age ago
dad spent a summer
weekend as a scout:

do random atoms—his—
still hover in this place—
sift through filtered air
to touch my face
across the vastnesses of time
and strictures of his narrow space?

motes of memory
brushed by at 65
adance in a fading sun
without embrace

Dusk

Toward evening,
Shawled in sun's last rays,
I watch for moonrise
Over darkened hills
And silvered beams
To light my shadowed way.

Four Questions[3]

When I enter at the narrow door,
will you teach me as before
(guiding finger long since gone to bone)
page on flaking page of ancient lore
in antique alphabet: kometz-aleph-aw?

Drape a faded tallis shred by shred
about my shoulders and my head?

Wrap withered strips of leather round my arm
to perish at the finger and the palm?

Yet, how should we meet, my zayde,
reft of sense and breath,
in that airless, unlit, silent cheder?

Legacies

After the last breath—
Lids lowered
Mouth fixed
A last cold kiss—
All (else)
Unmoving
Silence seems:
Now as nails or hair
Still grow
The sputter and hiss
(somewhere)
of restless
unextinguished dreams

————

Notes

[1]On July 20, 1944 Claus von Stauffenberg led a failed attempt to assassinate Adolph Hitler by means of an explosive device attached to a conference table. He and other officers complicit in the attempt were executed by firing squad the following day.

[2]Convicted in Utah and sentenced to death for first-degree murder, Gary Gilmore was executed by firing squad in January, 1977. He chose the method over hanging, his other option. Post sentencing, Gilmore rejected all appeals attempted on his behalf. The firing squad was selected from local law enforcement volunteers.

As the first execution carried out in the United States in ten years, owing to a Supreme Court ruling later reversed, the event received great attention, again stirring up debate over capital punishment.

Quotations in the text are as reported by the press or nearly so. The Latin dialogue in 6 was initiated by Gilmore and addressed to the Roman Catholic priest who had administered the last rites.

Section 13 suggests the televising of executions, a possibility sometimes discussed. Gilmore's was not televised, but the event was heavily covered by both electronic and print news outlets, whose reporters and crews were gathered outside the prison along with citizens who had come either to support or oppose the execution.

[3]The title here alludes to the four questions asked by children at the Passover seder, the answers to which refer to the exodus from Egypt.

A "kometz" is one of the diacritical marks used in Hebrew to indicate vowel sounds, since the alphabet proper lacks them.

A "tallis" is usually referred to in English as a prayer shawl. But the garment does not necessarily cover the head and might cover more than the shoulders.

"Strips of leather" are extensions of the phylacteries worn at weekday morning services.

"Zayde" is the Yiddish word for grandfather.

"Cheder" is a Hebrew school.

Acknowledgements

The poems listed below appeared previously
in the publications noted.

"swimmer" (in "homages to hopper"), "The Reading," and
"Antiphon" in *Poetry Newsletter* No. 22 (September 1973).

"Occupational Hazard" in *The Barefoot Muse* (Spring/
Summer 2006) and *TheHyperTexts* (Fall 2006).

"Mutual Reflection" in *The Lyric* (May 2004).

"Pas de Deux" in *Salome* (Summer 1982).

"Dear Walt," in *The Mickle Street Review* (1980).

9 798995 712916